Mark tells us the Good News about Jesus

An EasyEnglish Bible Book

Bible Society

Bible Society
Trinity Business Centre
Stonehill Green, Westlea
Swindon SN5 7DG
biblesociety.org.uk
bibleresources.org.uk

EasyEnglish Gospel of Mark
ISBN 978 0 564 04793 2

Typography and typesetting by Bible Society Resources Ltd,
a wholly-owned subsidiary of The British and Foreign Bible Society
Cover design by Patrick Knowles
Production arranged by Bible Society Resources Ltd

EEGMARK/BSRL/2022/0.25M
Printed in the United Kingdom

CONTENTS

Mark tells us the Good News about Jesus

A word list at the end explains words with a star[*] by them

This is about the book that Mark wrote

Mark wrote this book while he was living in Rome. Rome is now the capital city of Italy. He wrote it at some time between AD 50* and AD 70*. Mark was also called John Mark. He was a young man when Jesus was on earth. In the book called Acts, we can read some things about Mark. A group of Christians met together in the home of Mark's mother (Acts 12:12). Paul and Barnabas went to many different places to tell people about Jesus. And sometimes, Mark went with them.

Mark wrote his book for people who were not Jews*. At that time, the Roman* government, which ruled many countries in the world, was hurting Christians. Jesus had said that men would hurt his people. Mark wanted to tell everyone about the things that Jesus had done. He described how Jesus lived. He explained who Jesus was. Jesus was a man, but he was also God's son. Mark described how Jesus died on a cross*. And he described how Jesus became alive again. He explained how people could let God rule in their lives. He wrote about the things that Jesus taught the people.

Mark was a friend of Peter. Peter was one of the 12 men that Jesus chose to be his disciples*. He called them apostles*. Mark often listened when Peter was talking about Jesus. He wrote down the things that Peter said. And he wrote about the things that he had seen himself.

This is a list of the different parts of Mark's book:

1 Jesus starts his work 1:1–13
2 Jesus works in Galilee 1:14—9:50
3 Jesus travels from Galilee to Jerusalem 10:1–10:52
4 In Jerusalem, people kill Jesus and his friends bury him
   11:1—15:47
5 Jesus becomes alive again 16:1-8
6 People see that Jesus is alive 16:9-20

Jerusalem is now the capital city of Israel* and Galilee is part
of Israel*.

MARK

1

The start of the good news

¹This is the start of the good news about Jesus Christ. He is the Son of God. ²Isaiah wrote this message from God in his book:

'I will send someone in front of you. He will speak my message.

He will prepare a way for you.'
³ 'A voice is shouting in the wilderness*:

"The Lord* will come soon. So prepare a road for him to travel on.

Make the paths straight."'

⁴So John came to a place in the wilderness* with the message from God. 'You have done many wrong things', he taught everybody. 'You must change your minds. Then God will forgive* you and I will baptise* you.'

⁵Many people who lived in Jerusalem city and in the country called Judea went to listen to John. The people told God about all the wrong things that they had done. Then John baptised* the people in the river Jordan. ⁶John wore clothes that he had made out of hair from a camel*. He also wore a belt that he had made from the skin of an animal. His usual food was large insects and honey* from the wilderness*.

⁷'A person will come soon', John said to the people. 'He is more important than I am. I should not even be the servant who undoes his shoes. ⁸I have baptised* you with water. But this other person will baptise* you with the Holy* Spirit.'

John baptises* Jesus

9 Soon after this, Jesus came from the town called Nazareth in Galilee. John baptised* him in the river Jordan. 10 While Jesus was coming up out of the water, the skies seemed to open. The Holy* Spirit came down like a bird and he rested on Jesus. 11 A voice spoke from the sky. That voice said, 'You are my son and I love you. You make me very happy.'

Satan* tries to cause Jesus to do wrong things

12 Immediately, the Holy* Spirit sent Jesus out into the wilderness*. 13 He was in the wilderness* for 40 days. During this time, Satan* tried to cause Jesus to do wrong things. There were wild animals near to Jesus in the wilderness*. And God's angels* were his servants.

Jesus asks some men to be his disciples*

14 When John was in a prison, Jesus went to Galilee. He told people the good news about God. 15 'Now is the time when God will begin to rule his people', Jesus said. 'You have done many wrong things. You must change your minds. Believe the Good News.'

16 On one day, Jesus was walking along the shore of Lake Galilee. He saw two brothers called Simon and Andrew. Their job was to catch fish. They were throwing their nets* into the lake to catch fish. 17 'Come with me', Jesus said to them. 'I will teach you how to catch people.' 18 Simon and Andrew immediately left their nets* and they went with Jesus.

19 Then Jesus continued to walk along the shore. Soon he saw two more men who were brothers. They were called James and John. They were the sons of Zebedee. They were in their boat and they were mending their nets*. 20 Immediately, Jesus asked them to come with him. They left their father and his workers in the boat. And they went with Jesus.

Jesus causes a bad spirit* to leave a man

21 Then Jesus and those disciples* went into Capernaum. On
the next Jewish* day for rest, Jesus went into the meeting
place. He began to teach the people there.

22 Jesus taught the people very well. He taught with authority
and that surprised them. He was not like the teachers of God's
rules, because they did not speak with authority. 23 In the
meeting place, there was a man who had a bad spirit*. The bad
spirit* caused the man to shout loudly. 24 'Jesus from Nazareth',
it said, 'We have nothing in common! Do not kill us! I know
who you are. You are holy* and you have come from God.'

25 Jesus spoke to the bad spirit*. 'Be quiet!' he said. 'Come
out of the man!' 26 The bad spirit* caused the man to fall. It
shouted loudly and then it came out of the man.

27 All the people were very surprised, and they said to each
other, 'This is very strange. Jesus is teaching us something
new and he speaks with authority. He can say to bad spirits*
what they must do. And they obey him.' 28 Immediately, people
began to tell the news about Jesus. Everywhere in Galilee,
they were telling other people about him.

Jesus makes many people well

29 Then Jesus left the meeting place. He took James and
John with him to the home of Simon and Andrew. 30 The
mother of Simon's wife was ill in bed. Her body was very hot.
Immediately, Simon and Andrew told Jesus about her. 31 So he
went to her and he held her hand. Then he helped her to sit
up and immediately she was well. Then she prepared food for
Jesus and for his disciples*.

32-33 That evening, when the sun had gone down, everybody
in the town came. They brought to Jesus everyone who was
ill. And they brought people with bad spirits*. All these people
were round the door of the house. 34 Jesus caused many sick

people to become well. They had many different illnesses. He also caused many bad spirits* to leave people. The spirits* knew who he was. So Jesus did not let them speak.

Jesus prays alone in a quiet place

35 Jesus got up very early the next morning, while it was still dark. He went to a place where he could be alone. And there he prayed. 36 Simon and the other disciples* had to look for him. 37 When they found him, they said, 'Everyone is looking for you.'

38 'We should go to some other place', Jesus replied. 'We will go to other towns near here, so that I can teach the people there also. I came here for that reason.' 39 So Jesus travelled everywhere in Galilee. He taught the people in their meeting places. He caused bad spirits* to come out of people.

A man with an illness in his skin

40 On one day, a man who had an illness in his skin came to Jesus. He went down on his knees in front of Jesus. The man said. 'If you want to do it, you can make me well again.'

41 Jesus felt very sorry for the man. He moved his hand towards the man and he touched the man. 'I do want to help you', Jesus said. 'Be well!' 42 Immediately, the illness left the man and his skin was clean.

43 Jesus explained carefully to the man and he sent him away immediately. 44 'Listen. Do not tell anyone about this', Jesus said. 'But go and show yourself to the priest*. Take a gift to him for God. Moses taught the people what gift to take to God after this kind of illness. This will show other people that you are now well.' 45 But instead, the man went away and he talked to everybody. He told them what had happened to him. Because he did this, it became too difficult for Jesus to go into the towns. Everybody knew him, and so Jesus stayed in places in the wilderness*. And the people came from every direction to see him.

2

Jesus helps a man who cannot walk

[1] Jesus returned to Capernaum several days after that. People reported that he had come back to his home. [2] Many people came into the house. The house was so full that there was no room, even outside the door. Jesus was teaching the people. [3] Four men came. They were carrying another man, who could not walk. [4] They could not reach Jesus because of the crowd. So they made a hole in the roof above the place where Jesus was. They helped the man to go down through the hole. The man was still lying on his small carpet. [5] Jesus saw the man and his friends. And he knew that they believed. So he said to the man, 'My friend, I forgive* you for the wrong things that you have done.'

[6] But some teachers of God's rules were sitting there. They thought about the words that Jesus had spoken to the man. [7] 'This man (Jesus) should not have said that', they thought. 'He is speaking as only God can speak. Only God can forgive* people for the wrong things that they have done.'

[8] Immediately, Jesus knew what the teachers were thinking. 'You should not think these things', he said to them. [9] 'I said to this man, "I forgive* you for the wrong things that you have done." Instead, I might have said to him, "Stand up! Pick up your small carpet and walk." You know which is easier to say. [10] But I want you to know this. I, the Son* of Man, have authority on earth. I can forgive* people for the wrong things that they have done.' Then he spoke to the man who could not walk. [11] 'I am saying to you: Stand up! Pick up your small carpet and go to your home.' [12] The man stood up. Immediately, he picked up the small carpet. Everyone watched him walk out of the house. This surprised all the people very much. The people said that God had done this powerful thing. They said, 'We have never seen anything like this before.'

Jesus asks Levi to be his disciple*

13 Jesus went back to the shore of Lake Galilee. A large crowd came to him, so he taught them. 14 While Jesus was walking along, he saw Levi. Levi was the son of Alphaeus. His job was to take money on behalf of the government. He was sitting in his office. 'Come with me', Jesus said to him. Levi stood up and he went with Jesus.

15 Then Jesus went to eat a meal at Levi's house. Many people followed Jesus and they ate there with him and with his disciples*. Some of these people also took money on behalf of the government. Some of the people had done many wrong things. 16 Some teachers of God's rules saw Jesus while he was eating with all those people. They said to his disciples*, 'Jesus should not eat with men who take money on behalf of the Roman* government. And he should not eat with those other bad people.'

17 Jesus heard what the teachers of God's rules said. 'People who are well do not need a doctor', he answered them. 'People who are ill need a doctor. I did not come to help good people. I came to help bad people.'

18 At this time, the disciples* of John the Baptist* and the disciples* of the Pharisees* were not eating any food. Some people came to Jesus and they asked him this question. 'The disciples* of John and the disciples* of the Pharisees* are not eating any food. So why are your disciples* eating food?'

19 Jesus said to them, 'When a man marries, his friends cannot refuse to eat. They cannot refuse food while he is with them. 20 But there will be a time when people will take him away from them. Then his friends will refuse food.'

21 Jesus said, 'Nobody uses a piece of new cloth to mend an old coat. If he does, the new cloth will cause the old cloth to tear again. It will make a bigger hole than before. 22 And nobody pours new wine* into old wineskins*. If he does, the

new wine* will tear the old wineskins*. He will lose the wine* and the wineskins*. Instead, you must put new wine* into new wineskins*.'

Jesus answers questions about the day when people should rest

23 On one Jewish* day for rest, Jesus and his disciples* were walking through the fields where wheat* was growing. His disciples* picked some wheat* seeds. 24 Some Pharisees* said to Jesus, 'Look at your disciples*! They are doing what they should not do on the day for rest. It is against the rules.'

25 'Remember what David did', Jesus replied. 'He and the men with him were very hungry. You have read about this. 26 David went into God*'s Great House. He ate the special bread from there. And he gave it to the men who were with him. This happened during the life of Abiathar, who was the most important priest*. It is against God's rules for anyone except the priests* to eat this special bread.'

27 Then Jesus said to the Pharisees*, 'God wanted to help people. So he made the day when they should rest. He did not make people so that there would be a day to rest. 28 So, the Son* of Man even has authority over the day when people should rest.'

3

Jesus makes a man well

1 Again, Jesus went into the meeting place. A man was there. His hand was very small and weak and he could not use it. 2 Some Pharisees* were watching Jesus carefully. They wanted to find a reason to say that Jesus was doing wrong things. It was the day when people should rest. So the Pharisees* watched to see if Jesus would make the man well on this day. 3 Jesus said to the man, 'Stand here in front of everyone.'

4 Then Jesus said to the Pharisees*, 'What can we do on our day for rest? What do the rules say? Do they say that we

should do good things? Or do they say that we should do bad things? Should we save a person's life? Or should we kill?'

Nobody said anything.

5 Jesus looked round at everybody. He felt angry with them. He also felt sad because they did not want to change their minds. Then he said to the man, 'Lift your hand.' The man lifted it and his hand became well. 6 Then the Pharisees* left the building immediately. They met a group of people who wanted to obey Herod. And they talked with them about how they could kill Jesus.

Crowds follow Jesus

7 Jesus left that place and he went away to Lake Galilee with his disciples*. A large crowd from Galilee followed them. 8 Many people also came to him from Judea, Jerusalem and a part of Israel called Idumea. They came from places on the other side of the river Jordan. And they came from the towns called Tyre and Sidon. People were telling the news about the things that Jesus was doing. That is why all these people came. 9 The crowd was very large. So Jesus asked his disciples* to prepare a small boat for him. They did this so that the people would not push against him. 10 Sick people pushed to the front, because they were trying to touch him. They knew that he had made many people well. 11 Often, a person with a bad spirit* saw Jesus. Then, the spirit* caused the person to fall down on the ground in front of Jesus. The spirit* caused that person to shout out, 'You are the Son of God.' 12 Jesus often had to say to the bad spirits*, 'You must not tell anyone who I am.'

Jesus chooses 12 apostles*

13 Jesus went up a mountain. He chose some men and he asked them to go there with him. So they met him there. 14 He chose a group of 12 men who would be his apostles*. He wanted them to be with him. And he would send them to teach people about

God. ¹⁵He gave these men authority to cause bad spirits* to leave people. ¹⁶These are the names of the 12 apostles*:
　　Simon, whom Jesus called Peter,
¹⁷ James and John who were the sons of Zebedee. Jesus called them 'Boanerges'. It means 'men who are like a loud noise in a storm',
¹⁸ Andrew,
　　Philip,
　　Bartholomew,
　　Matthew,
　　Thomas,
　　James, who was the son of Alphaeus,
　　Thaddaeus,
　　Simon the Zealot*
¹⁹ and Judas Iscariot. He delivered Jesus to the people who were against him.

Jesus talks about Satan*

²⁰Then Jesus went into a house. And again, a crowd came to the house. There were so many people that Jesus and his disciples* were not even able to eat. ²¹People told his family* what was happening. So they went to take him away with them. They thought that Jesus was crazy.

²²Some teachers of God's rules came from Jerusalem. 'Jesus has a bad spirit* called Beelzebul', they said. ' Satan* rules all the bad spirits*. So Satan* has given authority to Jesus. That is how Jesus causes the bad spirits* to come out of people.'

²³So Jesus spoke to the teachers of God's rules. 'Come here and listen', he said to them. He used stories to explain to them. ' Satan* would not fight against himself! ²⁴If armies in the same country start to fight each other, then they will destroy their own country. ²⁵And if the people in one family start to fight against each other, they will destroy their own family. ²⁶So Satan* would not fight against himself. If he did, he would destroy his own power*. That would be his end. ²⁷Nobody can easily go into the house of a strong man to rob him. To do that,

he must first tie up the strong man. Then he can take away
all that man's valuable things. ²⁸What I say to you is true.
God can forgive* all the wrong things that people do. He can
also forgive* people who say bad things about him. ²⁹But God
will never forgive* people who say bad things about the Holy*
Spirit. They will always be guilty*.'

³⁰Jesus said this to the teachers of God's rules, because they
said, 'Jesus has a bad spirit*.'

Jesus' mother and his brothers come to look for him

³¹Then, Jesus' mother and his brothers arrived and they stood
outside the house. They sent someone with a message. They
wanted Jesus to come to them. ³²A crowd was sitting round
Jesus. They said to him, 'Look! Your mother and brothers are
outside. They are looking for you.'

³³Jesus answered, 'I will tell you who my mother and brothers
really are.'

³⁴Then he looked at the people who were sitting round him in a
circle. 'Look! Here are my mother and brothers! ³⁵My brothers
and sisters and mother are those people who obey God',
said Jesus.

4

Jesus tells a story about a farmer's seeds

¹Again, Jesus began to teach by Lake Galilee. The crowd that
came together was very large. So, he climbed into a boat and
he sat down. The boat was in the water, and the people stayed
on the shore. ²Jesus used stories to teach them many things.
³'Listen to me', said Jesus. 'A farmer went out to plant seeds.
⁴While he was planting the seeds, some seeds fell on the path.
The birds came and they ate those seeds. ⁵Other seeds fell
among the rocks. There was a little soil* in that place. The
seeds quickly began to grow, because the soil* was not deep.
⁶But when the sun rose, it burned the young plants. They soon

died because they had not grown down into the soil*. 7Other seeds fell among bushes with sharp branches. Those bushes grew up with the young plants. The bushes were stronger than the farmer's plants. So the plants could not make any new seeds. 8But some seeds fell on good soil*. Good strong plants grew from these seeds. Some plants made 30 new seeds. Some plants made 60 new seeds. And some plants made 100 new seeds.'

9Then Jesus said, 'You have heard my words. So do what I say.'

Jesus explains to his disciples* why he uses stories

10When Jesus was alone, his friends and the 12 disciples* asked him about the story. 11'God has let you understand how he rules his people', Jesus replied. 'But the other people listen to stories. 12This is so that:
   "They are looking and looking. But they do not see.
   They are listening and listening. But they do
      not understand."

If they did understand, they would obey God. And if they did obey God, he would forgive* them.'

Jesus explains the story about the seeds

13Then Jesus answered the people who had asked him about the story. 'You should understand this story. If you do not understand it, you will not understand all the other stories. 14The seeds mean the message from God. The farmer is like a person who teaches people about that message. 15Some seeds fell on the path. The path is like some people who listen to the message. But then Satan* comes quickly to them. And he takes the message away from their minds. 16Some of the seeds fell among rocks. This is like some people who listen to the message from God. They are happy to believe it for a time. 17But they are like plants that have not grown into the soil*. So they will only believe for a short time. They may have problems. Or other people may do bad things to them because of God's message. The result is that those people stop believing. ¹⁸Some seeds fell among bushes that had sharp branches. This is like some other people who listen to the message from God. ¹⁹But they have many troubles in their minds. They think that more money and other valuable things will make them happy. So they do not let God's message change them. They are like plants that do not make new seeds. ²⁰But some seeds fell on good soil*. This soil* is like other people who listen to the message from God. They understand it and they obey God. These people are like good plants. From one seed, the good plants make 30 seeds. Other good plants make 60 new seeds, and some good plants make 100 new seeds.'

People put a light in a high place

²¹Then Jesus said to his disciples*, 'Nobody brings a lamp* into a house and puts it under a jar or under a bed. You do not do that. You put it in a high place. ²²God hides some things now. But there will be a time when people will see them. God covers some things now because he does not want people to see them yet. But there will be a time when people will see all those things.' ²³Then Jesus said, 'You have heard my words. So do what I say.'

²⁴'You should be careful about how you listen', said Jesus. 'God will give to you in the way that you give to other people. And you will receive even more. ²⁵A person who has some things will receive more. Some people do not have those things. They will lose even the little bit that they do have.'

Jesus tells a story about seeds

²⁶Then Jesus said, 'I will explain how God rules his people. A man throws seeds in his field. ²⁷Then he sleeps each night and he wakes each day. The seeds start to grow into plants. They continue to grow, but the man does not know how. ²⁸The soil* causes the plants to grow. The leaves of the plant grow first. Then the flower appears, and then the seeds appear. ²⁹When

the plants have completely grown, the man will cut them down immediately. It is time for him to take the seeds to use for food.'

Jesus tells a story about a very small seed

30 'We should describe how God rules his people', said Jesus. 'I will explain it with another story. 31 It is like this. A man takes a seed of the plant called mustard. He puts it in the soil*. It is smaller than any other seed that is in the soil*. 32 But when it starts to grow, it becomes bigger than the largest bush. It will have big branches. And the birds will come from the sky and they will live there. They will build their homes in the shade of the branches.'

33 Jesus taught God's message to the people. He used many stories like these. He told the people as much as they could understand. 34 He always used stories to teach the people. Then he explained everything to his own disciples* when he was alone with them.

Jesus stops a storm

35 On that same day, in the evening, Jesus spoke to his disciples*. 'We should go across to the other side of the lake', he said. 36 So they left the crowd. Jesus was already in the boat. So the disciples* took him across the lake. Some other boats also went with them. 37 Then a strong wind began to blow across the lake. Water began to fill the boat so that soon the boat was almost under the water. 38 Jesus was in a comfortable place at the back of the boat. He was asleep. The disciples* woke Jesus, and they said to him, 'Teacher, it seems not to matter to you if we die!'

39 Jesus woke and he spoke to the wind and to the water. 'Be quiet!' he said. 'Stop!' Then the wind stopped and the water became flat again.

40 'You should not be afraid like that', Jesus said to his disciples*. 'You should believe.'

41 Then they were very afraid. 'We do not know who Jesus really is', they said to each other. 'Even the wind and the water obey him.'

5

Jesus meets a man who has many bad spirits* inside him

1 Jesus and his disciples* came to the other side of the lake. They came to a place near Gerasa.

2-4 Jesus came out of the boat. And immediately a man met him. A bad spirit* was living inside this man. So the man lived in a place where there were many human bones. Nobody could hold him. Often people tried to put metal round his ankles. They wanted to keep him in a safe place. But they all failed. He broke the metal. 5 The man was always either by the bones or on the hills. During each day and each night, he screamed. And he used stones to cut himself.

6 He saw Jesus a long way away and he ran to meet him. He went down on his knees in front of Jesus. 7 He screamed loudly, 'Jesus, we have nothing in common. You are the Son of the powerful God above. Please promise God that you will not hurt me.' 8 He said that because Jesus had already said to the bad spirit*, 'Come out of this man.'

9 Then Jesus asked the man, 'What is your name?'

The man replied, 'My name is Army because there are so many bad spirits* in me.'

10 He said to Jesus many times, 'Please do not send these bad spirits* out of this country.'

11 A large group of pigs was eating on the hill. 12 'Jesus, send us to the pigs. Let us go into them', said the bad spirits*. 13 Jesus let them. So, the bad spirits* came out of the man and they went into the pigs. All the pigs rushed together down the hill into the lake. About 2000 pigs died in the lake.

¹⁴The men who were feeding these pigs ran away. They told
the people in the town and in the farms. Those people came
to see what had happened. ¹⁵When they came to Jesus, they
saw the man. The man was now sitting quietly. The bad spirits*
had gone out of him. He was wearing clothes and his mind was
well again. This was the man that the army of bad spirits* had
ruled. All the people were afraid. ¹⁶The men who saw these
events spoke to them. They told the other people what had
happened to the man with the bad spirits*. And they explained
about the pigs. ¹⁷Then the people who lived there said to Jesus,
'Please leave our country.'

¹⁸Jesus climbed back into the boat. But the man that the
bad spirits* had ruled spoke to him. He told Jesus that he
very much wanted to be with him. ¹⁹But Jesus did not let
him. Instead, Jesus said to him, 'Go to your home and to your
friends. Tell them what the Lord* has done for you. Tell them
how he has been kind to you.' ²⁰So the man went away. He
began to speak to many people in the 10 cities there. He told
them about the great things that Jesus had done for him. And
all the people were very surprised.

Jesus makes a dead girl alive again

²¹So Jesus returned in the boat. He came to the other side of
the lake. A large crowd came to him there. And he was by the
lake. ²²A man called Jairus came to Jesus. He was a leader at
the meeting place. When he saw Jesus, he went down on his
knees. ²³'Please, please come to my house and put your hands
on my little daughter', he said to Jesus. 'She is very ill and
she will soon die. But if you do this, she will live.' ²⁴So Jesus
started to go with Jairus.

A large crowd followed Jesus. And the people were pushing
against him. ²⁵There was a sick woman who had bled for 12
years. ²⁶She had paid many doctors to help her, but they could
not do anything. They had caused her more pain instead.
Now she had spent all her money and she had not become

any better. Instead, she became worse. ²⁷People had told her about the things that Jesus did. So, she came in the crowd behind him and she touched his coat. ²⁸She said, 'Even if I can only touch his clothes, I will become well again.' ²⁹And immediately, the blood stopped. And she knew that she was well again.

³⁰Jesus knew immediately that something powerful had gone from him. So he turned round in the crowd and he asked, 'Who touched my clothes?'

³¹'You can see that the crowd is pushing against you', said his disciples*. 'You cannot ask who touched you!'

³²But Jesus looked round him. He wanted to see who had touched him. ³³The woman knew what had happened to her. And she felt very afraid. But she came to Jesus. And she went down on her knees. Then she told him everything that had happened to her. ³⁴'Young woman, do not have troubles in your mind', said Jesus. 'You are well again because you believed. Go now and be well.'

³⁵While Jesus was still speaking, some men arrived from Jairus's house. (Jairus was a leader at the meeting place.) 'Your daughter is dead', they said to Jairus. 'Do not ask any longer for the teacher to come.'

³⁶Jesus heard what the men said to Jairus. So Jesus said to him, 'Do not be afraid. Instead, believe.'

³⁷Jesus took only Peter, James and John (James's brother) with him. He would not let anyone else go with him. ³⁸Then they came to Jairus's house. And Jesus saw that there were many people there. They were all crying. They were making a loud noise. ³⁹Jesus went into the house and he said to the people, 'You should not be crying and making a loud noise. The child is not dead. She is asleep.' ⁴⁰The people laughed* at him.

Then Jesus sent them all out. He went into the place where the child was lying. The child's father and mother were with him. He also took Peter, James and John with him. ⁴¹Then Jesus held the little girl's hand. 'Talitha koum', he said to her. This means, 'Little girl, I ask you to stand up.' ⁴²The little girl stood up immediately and she walked about. She was 12 years old. They were very surprised. ⁴³'You must not tell anyone what has happened here', Jesus said to them. 'Now give the little girl something to eat.'

6

Jesus goes to his own town

¹Jesus left there. He came to his own town. His disciples* followed him.

²When it was the Jewish* day for rest, Jesus went to the meeting place. He began to teach the many people who were there. They were very surprised about the things that he was saying to them. 'We do not know how this man learned these things', they said to each other. 'We do not know how he knows so much. And we do not know how he does all these powerful things. ³We know who this man is. He is the carpenter*. He is the son of Mary. He is the brother of James, Joses, Simon and Judas. His sisters live here in the town among us.' This was the problem that they had with him.

⁴'People everywhere may speak well about a servant of God. But the people in that man's own town will not do that', Jesus said to them. 'His own people and his own family* will not speak well about him.'

⁵Jesus could not do any powerful thing in that town. But he did put his hands on a few sick people and he made them well. ⁶Jesus was very surprised because the people in that town would not believe.

Then he travelled through the villages that were round there in a circle. He was teaching the people in the villages.

Jesus sends the 12 disciples* to tell
God's message to people

⁷Jesus asked his 12 disciples* to come to him. He started to send pairs of them to tell God's message to people. And he gave them authority over bad spirits*.

⁸Jesus told the disciples* that they must not take anything for the journey, except only a stick. They must not take bread, a bag or money in their pockets. ⁹They should wear shoes. But they should not take extra clothes.

¹⁰Jesus said to them, 'In each town, stay at the first house that you go into. Continue to stay there until you leave that town. ¹¹Perhaps you might go to a town where the people do not accept you. They will not listen to you. So you should leave that town. Clean that town's dirt off your feet. So then it will be clear that they have done something wrong.'

¹²So they went out. They told the people that they must change their minds. ¹³They caused many bad spirits* to come out of people. They also put oil on many sick people; and the sick people became well.

Herod kills John the Baptist*

¹⁴People told King Herod about these things. People were talking about Jesus. Some people were saying that Jesus was John the Baptist*. They also said that John had become alive again. 'That is why Jesus does these very powerful things', they said.

¹⁵Other people said, 'Jesus is Elijah.' And other people said, 'He is a servant of God. He is like God's servants who lived a long time ago.'

¹⁶But when someone told Herod, he said, 'This is John. I sent a soldier to cut off his head. But John has become alive again!'

17Herod himself had sent his soldiers to take hold of John. He had said to his soldiers, 'Tie ropes* round John's hands and feet and put him in a prison.' Herod had done that because of Herodias. She was the wife of Herod's brother Philip. But Herod had married her. 18John had said to him, 'Herodias is your brother's wife. It is against the rules for you to have her as your wife.'

19Herodias was very much against John. So she wanted to kill him. But she could not do that. 20That was because Herod was afraid of John. Herod knew that John was a good man. And Herod knew that John was a servant of God. So Herod kept John safe. Herod liked to listen to what John said. But he did not know what to do about the things that John said.

21Then, on one day, Herodias had her chance. It was Herod's birthday and he asked many people to come to a special meal. Important men and officers came. And the rulers from Galilee were also there. 22The daughter of Herodias came in and she danced. Herod and his visitors were very happy when they saw her dance.

'Ask me for anything that you want', the king said to the young woman. 'I will give it to you.' 23And he promised: 'What I say is completely true. I will give you anything that you ask me to give to you. I will even give you half of all that I rule over.'

24The young woman went out and she said to her mother, 'What should I ask him for?' 'Ask for the head of John the Baptist*', her mother replied.

25The young woman returned quickly and she spoke immediately to Herod. 'I want the head of John the Baptist*. Put it on a plate! Do it now!'

26Then Herod felt very sad. But he did not want to disappoint her, because of his promise. All his visitors had heard it. 27So, immediately, the king sent a soldier. The king told the soldier that he must bring John's head. So, the soldier went to the prison and he cut off John's head there. 28Then he brought it back on a plate. He gave it to the young woman. And the young woman gave it to her mother. ²⁹People told John's disciples* about it. So, they went to the prison and they took away John's dead body. And then they buried it.

Jesus gives food to 5000 men and to their families

³⁰The apostles* all came to Jesus. They told him about all the things that they had done. And they told him what they had taught. ³¹Many people were coming and going. Jesus and the disciples* were too busy even to eat. So Jesus said to them, 'Come with me to a place where there are no other people. We should be alone together. Then we can rest for a short time.'

³²So they left the crowd. They went away in a boat together. They went into the wilderness*. ³³But many people saw that they were leaving the town. Those people recognised them. So they ran out from all the towns. And they reached the place before Jesus and the disciples* arrived. ³⁴Jesus climbed out of the boat and he saw a large crowd. Jesus felt sorry for them. He thought to himself, 'They are like sheep that have nobody to lead them.' So, he began to teach them many things.

³⁵When it was almost evening, Jesus' disciples* came to speak to him. 'We are here in a place in the wilderness*', they said. 'Soon it will be dark. ³⁶The people do not have anything to eat. So, send the crowd away now. Ask them to go to the farms and villages that are near here. There they can buy some food for themselves.'

³⁷'Give them some food to eat. You should do it', Jesus replied.

So the disciples* said, 'We cannot go to buy bread for the people. A man must work for 8 months to get the 200 coins that we would need. We cannot give food to these people.'

³⁸Jesus asked them, 'How many loaves of bread do you have? Go and see.' When they had looked, they spoke to Jesus again. 'We have 5 loaves and 2 fishes', they said.

³⁹Jesus asked all the people to sit on the green grass. He wanted them to sit in large groups. ⁴⁰So the people sat down in groups. Each group had 50 or 100 people in it. ⁴¹Then Jesus took the 5 loaves and the 2 fishes. He looked up to God's home, called heaven. And he thanked God for the food. Then he broke the bread into pieces. He gave the pieces of bread to the disciples*. And they gave the bread to the people. Jesus also broke the two fishes into pieces for all the people. ⁴²Everyone ate and they all had enough food. ⁴³Jesus' disciples* then picked up all the food that the people had not eaten. And they filled 12 baskets with pieces of bread and fish. ⁴⁴About 5000 men ate the loaves.

Jesus walks on water

⁴⁵Immediately, Jesus told his disciples* that they must get into the boat. They should go to Bethsaida, which is on the other side of the lake. Jesus would go there after some time. But first, he would send the crowd away. ⁴⁶So he said 'Goodbye' to the crowd. Then he went up a mountain to pray.

⁴⁷That evening, the boat was in the middle of the lake. Jesus was alone on the land. ⁴⁸But he could see his disciples*. They were trying to cause the boat to move along. But it was very difficult for them because the wind was blowing in the opposite direction. Then, when it was very early in the morning, Jesus came towards them. He was walking on the water. He wanted to pass them. ⁴⁹But they saw that he was walking on the water. 'It is a spirit*', they thought. And they screamed out. ⁵⁰They all saw him and they were afraid. But immediately, Jesus spoke with them. 'Be brave. It is I, Jesus. Do not be afraid', he said to them. ⁵¹Then Jesus climbed into the boat with them. The strong wind stopped. They were completely surprised about what had happened. ⁵²They did not understand what had happened to the loaves. And they were not ready to learn.

Jesus makes many sick people well

⁵³They crossed the lake. They reached the shore at
Gennesaret and they tied the boat there. ⁵⁴When they came
out of the boat, the people recognised Jesus immediately.
⁵⁵They went to tell everyone who lived anywhere near there.
They began to bring ill people to Jesus. They carried those ill
people to him on small carpets. They brought those people
to any place where he was. ⁵⁶Jesus went into villages, towns
and fields. Everywhere that he went, they brought sick people
into their market places to him. The sick people asked Jesus
for help. They wanted to touch even the edge of his coat. And
every sick person who touched him became well.

7

Jesus speaks to Pharisees* and to
some teachers of God's rules

¹A group of Pharisees* and some teachers of God's rules came
from Jerusalem. They came to talk with Jesus. ²They had
watched Jesus' disciples*. Some of the disciples* did not wash
their hands before a meal. Instead, they were eating their
food as other people eat. ³(The Pharisees* and all the Jews* do
not eat until they have washed their hands carefully. They do
this because of a rule that their leaders made many years ago.
⁴When they come from the market place, they must always
wash. Unless they do this, they cannot eat. Their leaders
had also given them rules about how to do other things. For
example, there are rules about how they should wash cups,
pots and metal jars.)

⁵The Pharisees* and the teachers of God's rules said to Jesus,
'Your disciples* do not obey the rules that our leaders made
many years ago. Your disciples* have not washed their hands.
They are eating their food as other people eat.'

6 Jesus said to the Pharisees* and to the teachers of God's
rules, 'What Isaiah said about you is true. You are hypocrites*.
He wrote down these words from God.

> "These people say good things about me,
>   but they do not really want to obey me.
> 7 They teach rules that men gave to them.
>   So they pray to me without any purpose."'

8 'You have stopped obeying God', Jesus said to them. 'Instead
you obey the rules that men gave to people many years ago.'

9 He said to them, 'You are very careful to refuse God's rules,
because then you can obey your own old rules! 10 For example,
Moses wrote, "You must love your father and your mother and
you must obey them." He also said, "A person should die if he
says bad things against his father or against his mother." 11 But
you teach that a person can say to his father or to his mother,
"I would have given these gifts to you. But I cannot because
I have given them to God instead." 12 Then, you let him do
nothing for his father or for his mother. 13 So you have obeyed
the rules that you received from your leaders many years ago.
And you do not do what God wants. And you do many other
things like that.'

14 Again, Jesus asked all the people to come near to him. 'Listen
to me', he said, 'so that you can understand these things.
15 God's people are different from other people. But they are
not different because of things from outside that go into their
bodies. It is because of the things that come from their minds.
16 You have heard my words. So do what I say.'

Jesus explains to his disciples* what he had taught

17 Jesus left the crowd and he went into a house. Then his
disciples* asked Jesus to explain what he had taught.

18 'I am surprised that you too are not able to understand', said
Jesus. 'It should be clear that God's people are not different
from other people because of their food. Food goes into a

person's body from outside. ¹⁹You know that food does not go into the mind of a person. First, it goes into his stomach and then it goes out of his body. So all foods are clean.'

²⁰And Jesus said, 'God's people are different from other people because of things that come from them. ²¹So, bad thoughts come from a man's mind. And then that man does wrong things. He might have sex when he should not do it. He might rob somebody. He might kill somebody. He might have sex with another man's wife. ²²He might want other people's things. He might be cruel to other people. He might want other people to believe things that are not true. He wants whatever things he can get. He thinks whatever thoughts he wants to think about people. He speaks whatever wrong words he wants to say. He thinks that he is very important. He thinks very silly things.

²³All these wrong things begin inside people's minds. They come out of those people. But God's people must be different from those people.'

Jesus travels out of Israel

²⁴After that, Jesus went away. He was near the city called Tyre. He went into a house. He did not want anyone to know that he was there. But it was not possible to keep this a secret. ²⁵Immediately, someone told a certain woman about Jesus. This woman had a daughter who had a bad spirit*. The woman came and she went down on her knees by Jesus' feet. ²⁶She was not a Jew*; her family* was from Syrophoenicia. She asked Jesus to cause the bad spirit* to go out of her daughter.

²⁷Jesus said to the woman, 'First, the children must eat all that they want. It is not right to take bread from the children. You should not throw the children's food to the dogs.'

²⁸The woman replied. She said to him, 'Yes sir. But small pieces of bread drop while the children eat. And the dogs under the table eat those pieces.'

²⁹'Because you have said that, you can go to your home', Jesus replied. 'Now the bad spirit* has left your daughter.'

³⁰The woman went to her home. She found the child, who was lying on the bed. The bad spirit* had left the child.

³¹Then Jesus went away from Tyre. He travelled through the city called Sidon. He went towards Lake Galilee. He was in the middle of the 10 cities there.

³²Some people brought a man to Jesus. This man could not hear and he could not speak clearly. The people asked Jesus to put his hand on the man.

³³Jesus led the man away from the crowd. Then he put his fingers into the man's ears. Then Jesus took water from his own mouth and he touched the man's tongue* with it. ³⁴Jesus looked up towards the sky. He made a low, sad sound. Then he said to the man, 'Ephphatha!' That means, 'Become open!' ³⁵Then the man started to hear. And immediately, the man's tongue* was able to move. And the man spoke clearly.

³⁶Jesus told the people that they must not tell anyone about this. But when Jesus asked them not to say anything, they spoke even more about it. ³⁷The people were very surprised about everything that Jesus did. 'Jesus has done everything well', they said. 'If people cannot hear, Jesus makes them able to hear. If people cannot speak, Jesus makes them able to speak.'

8

Jesus gives food to 4000 people

¹At that time, another large crowd had come to hear Jesus. The people had nothing to eat. Jesus asked his disciples* to come to him. Then he spoke to them. ²'I feel sorry for this crowd. They have been with me now for three days and they do not have any food. ³I do not want to send them back to their homes while they are hungry. They may fall down

during their journey because of weakness. Some of them have travelled a long way.'

⁴The disciples* replied, 'We are in the wilderness*. We cannot get enough bread to feed these people.'

⁵'How many loaves of bread do you have?' Jesus asked. 'We have 7 loaves', they replied.

⁶Jesus told the crowd that they should sit on the ground. Then he took the 7 loaves. He thanked God for them. Then he broke the bread and he gave the pieces to his disciples*. The disciples* gave the bread to the people. ⁷The disciples* also had a few small fishes, so Jesus thanked God for these. Then he told his disciples* that they should give the fishes to the people too. ⁸The people ate, and they all had enough food. After the people had eaten, there were still some pieces of bread and fish. Jesus' disciples* filled 7 baskets with these pieces. ⁹There were about 4000 people. And Jesus sent the people away. ¹⁰Immediately, he got into the boat with his disciples*. Then they all returned to the part of the country called Dalmanutha.

¹¹Some Pharisees* came. They began to argue with Jesus. They wanted him to do something powerful. They wanted him to show them that God had sent him. ¹²Jesus felt very sad. 'People today ask to see something powerful', he said. 'What I say is true. These people will not see the powerful thing that they want.' ¹³Then Jesus left the Pharisees* again. He got back into the boat to go to the other side of the lake.

Jesus talks about the yeast* of the Pharisees* and the yeast* of Herod

¹⁴Jesus' disciples* had forgotten to bring bread with them. They only had one loaf in the boat. ¹⁵'Be careful', Jesus said to them. 'You must watch for the yeast* of the Pharisees* and the yeast* of Herod.'

16 The disciples* began to talk to each other about this. 'Jesus is saying this because we do not have any bread', they said.

17 Jesus knew about this. So he said to them, 'You should not be talking about the fact that you do not have any bread. You still do not recognise or understand. You seem unable to learn. 18 You are like people who cannot see with their eyes. You are like people who cannot hear with their ears. Remember this! 19 I broke 5 loaves for 5000 men. How many baskets did you fill with pieces of bread?'

'There were 12 baskets', they replied.

20 'And then I broke 7 loaves for 4000 people. How many baskets did you fill with pieces of bread?' Jesus asked.

'There were 7 baskets', they replied.

21 'You should understand now', he said to them.

Jesus makes a blind* man able to see

22 Jesus and his disciples* came to a village called Bethsaida. Some people led a blind* man to Jesus. They asked Jesus to touch the man. 23 Jesus took the blind* man's hand and he led the man out of the village. Jesus put water from his own mouth on the man's eyes. And Jesus put his hands on the man. 'Can you see anything?' Jesus asked.

24 The man looked up. 'I can see people', he replied. 'But they seem like trees that are walking about.'

25 So Jesus put his hands on the man's eyes again. The man looked carefully and then his eyes were well. Now he could see everything clearly. 26 Jesus told the man that he must go back to his house. Jesus said, 'Do not even go into the village.'

Peter says who Jesus is

27 Then Jesus and his disciples* went to visit some villages. They were near to the town called Caesarea that Philip built. On the way, Jesus asked his disciples*, 'Who do people say that I am?'

28 'Some people say that you are John the Baptist*', they replied. 'Other people say that you are Elijah. And some other people say that you are one of God's servants.'

29 'But what do you think?' Jesus asked them. 'Who do you say that I am?'

'You are the Messiah*', Peter answered him.

30 Then Jesus spoke with authority to his disciples*. He said that they must not tell anybody about him.

Jesus tells his disciples* how he would die

31 Then Jesus began to teach his disciples* about the things that must happen to the Son* of Man. People would cause many troubles for him. Important people would be against him. They would include the important priests*, the leaders and the teachers of God's rules. People would kill him. But after three days, he would become alive again.

32 What Jesus said was very clear. Then Peter took Jesus away from the other disciples*. And Peter began to tell Jesus that he must not say those things.

33 But Jesus turned round and he saw his disciples*. And he said that Peter was wrong. ' Satan*, go away from me!' Jesus said to Peter. 'Your thoughts do not come from God. Instead, you are thinking like men think.'

34 Then Jesus asked the crowd and his disciples* to come to him. He said to them, 'A person who wants to be my disciple* must not think about himself. And he must not think about what he wants to do. He must decide that his own life is not important. And he must be like someone who carries his own cross*. Then he should become my disciple*. 35 The person who wants to save his life* will die. But another person may die because of me and because of God's good news. Even if that person dies, he will save his life*. 36 Think about a person who gets the whole world and everything in it. If he loses

his life*, he has not received anything. 37A man can receive nothing that is better than his life*. And all the money in the world cannot keep someone alive. 38People today do not obey God. They are very bad. But you must not be ashamed of me or of my words. If you are, the Son* of Man will be ashamed of you. He will be ashamed when he returns. On that day, the Son* of Man will shine because his Father is so beautiful. And God's holy* angels* will be with him.'

9

Three disciples* see how great Jesus is

1And Jesus said to them, 'What I am saying is true. Soon God will begin to rule his people with great power*. And some of the people who are standing here will see it. They will certainly not die before this happens.'

2Six days after that, Jesus asked Peter, James and John to go with him. Jesus led them up a high mountain, where they were alone together. And they saw Jesus as they had never seen him before. 3His clothes became very white; they were shining. They were a brighter white than anyone on earth could wash them. 4Then the three disciples* saw Elijah with Moses, who appeared to them. Elijah and Moses were talking with Jesus.

5So Peter said to Jesus, 'Teacher, it is good that we are here. Please let us build three huts. One hut will be for you. One hut will be for Moses. And one hut will be for Elijah.' 6Peter did not really know what to say. That was because the three disciples* had become very afraid.

7Then a cloud came. It covered them all. A voice spoke from the cloud. That voice said, 'This is my son, and I love him. Listen to him.'

8At that moment, the three disciples* looked round. They saw that nobody else was there still. Only Jesus was with them.

⁹While they were walking down the mountain again, Jesus said to the three disciples*, 'You must not tell anyone about the things that you saw. Tell people only after the Son* of Man has become alive after his death.' ¹⁰These disciples* kept these words secret. But they talked together about the words, 'alive after his death'. They wanted to understand those words.

¹¹Then the three disciples* asked Jesus, 'Why do the teachers of God's rules say that Elijah must come first?'

¹²Jesus said to them, 'Elijah does come first. He makes everything ready. But the Bible says that people will cause many troubles for the Son* of Man. People will do the worst things to him. ¹³But I tell you that Elijah has already come. People did to him whatever things they wanted to do. The Bible says that those things would happen to him.'

Jesus helps a boy who has a bad spirit*

¹⁴They reached the place where the other disciples* were. They saw that there was a large crowd round the disciples*. Some teachers of God's rules were arguing with them. ¹⁵The people in the crowd saw Jesus. And immediately they were very surprised. They ran to say 'hello' to Jesus.

¹⁶Jesus asked his disciples*, 'What were you arguing about with the teachers of God's rules?'

¹⁷A man in the crowd answered. He said to Jesus, 'Teacher, I brought my son to you. He is not able to speak because he has a bad spirit*. ¹⁸When the bad spirit* takes hold of him, it throws him to the ground. Water comes out of his mouth and he bites his teeth together. Then his body seems dead. I asked your disciples* to send the spirit* out of him. But they were not able to do it.'

¹⁹'You people today still do not believe', Jesus said to them. 'It is very difficult to be with you. I am always waiting for you to believe. Bring the boy to me.'

20 So the people brought the boy to Jesus. When the spirit* saw Jesus, it immediately caused the boy to fall badly. The boy fell on to the ground and he rolled about. Water was coming from his mouth.

21 'How long has he been like this?' Jesus asked the boy's father.

'He has been like this since he was a small boy', the father replied. 22 'Often the spirit* has caused him to fall into fire or into water. It is trying to kill him. But if you can do anything, be sorry for us. And help us!'

23 'You should not say, "If you can do anything"', Jesus said to the father. 'Everything is possible for those people who believe.'

24 Immediately, the boy's father shouted, 'Oh! I believe! Help me to believe more!'

25 Jesus saw that a crowd was running together again. So he told the bad spirit* that it must leave the boy. Jesus said to it, ' Spirit*, I am telling you that you must leave this boy. He cannot hear or speak because of you. But you must come out of him and you must never go into him again.'

26 The spirit* caused the boy to scream. It caused him to fall several times. Then it came out of him. The boy seemed to be dead. So, many people said, 'He is dead.' 27 But Jesus held the boy's hand and he helped the boy to stand up. So the boy stood up.

28 When Jesus went into a house, the disciples* were alone with him. Then they asked him, 'Why could we not cause the bad spirit* to leave the boy?'

29 'You must pray. No other thing can cause this kind of spirit* to go out of a person', said Jesus.

30 Jesus and his disciples* left that place. They passed through Galilee. Jesus did not want anyone to know where he was. 31 That was because he was teaching his disciples*. He told

them, 'Soon, someone will deliver the Son* of Man to a group
of men who will take him away. And they will kill him. And
three days after that, he will become alive again.' ³²The
disciples* did not understand what Jesus meant. And they
were afraid to ask him.

Jesus explains who will be the most important person

³³Jesus and his disciples* arrived at Capernaum. When they
were in the house, Jesus asked them, 'What were you arguing
about on the way?' ³⁴But they did not say anything. They did
not want to tell Jesus why they were arguing. On the way, they
had argued about who was the most important disciple*.

³⁵Jesus sat down. He asked the 12 disciples* to come. Then he
said to them, 'If you want to be the leader, make yourself less
important than everyone else. Become the servant of everyone.'

³⁶Then he took a child. He put that child in the middle of the
disciples*. While Jesus hugged the child, he said to them, ³⁷'If
someone accepts this child because of me, then he accepts me.
If he accepts me, then he is not only accepting me. He is also
accepting God, who sent me.'

³⁸'Teacher', John said to Jesus, 'we saw a man who is not in
our group. He was causing bad spirits* to go out of people.
And he was using your authority to do it. He is not in our
group. So we told him that he must not do it.'

³⁹'Do not tell him that', Jesus said. 'That man is using my
authority to do something powerful. Someone who does that
cannot soon say anything bad about me. ⁴⁰If someone is not
against us, he is helping us. ⁴¹Somebody may give you a cup of
water because you are a servant of the Messiah*. God will be
good to that person; he will not disappoint that person. What
I am saying is true.

⁴²A person who believes may not seem important. But you
should never cause that person to do wrong things. It would

be better if someone put a big stone round your neck. It would be better if someone then threw you into the sea!

43-44 If your hand causes you to do wrong things, you should cut it off. A person with only one hand can go to the place where God rules. That is better than to go to the place called hell*. There, the fire always burns. 45-46 If your foot causes you to do wrong things, you should cut it off. A person with only one foot can go to the place where God rules. That is better than to go to the place called hell*. 47 If your eye causes you to do wrong things, then you should take it out. A person with only one eye can go to the place where God rules. That is better than to go to the place called hell*.

48 "In hell*, the worms* do not die,
   and the fire never goes out."'

49 'God will put fire on everybody as people put salt on food.'

50 'Salt is good. But it must be salty. If your salt is not salty, you cannot make it salty. Be like good salt and love each other. Do not cause trouble among yourselves.'

10

Jesus teaches about men who send their wives away

1 Then Jesus left that place and he went to Judea. And he went to the east of the river Jordan. Large crowds came to him again. So he taught them as he had done before.

2 Some Pharisees* came to Jesus. They wanted to see how Jesus would answer their question. They asked, 'Can a man send his wife away, so that she is no longer his wife?'

3 Jesus answered them with a question. 'What rules did Moses write about this for you?'

4 The Pharisees* said, 'Moses said that a man could write a letter for his wife. The letter shows that the man and the woman are now separate. Then the man can send the woman away.'

5 'You did not want to obey God. That is why Moses made this rule for you', Jesus said to them. 6 'But at the start of the world, God made people male and female. 7 This is the reason that a man leaves his father and his mother. Then God joins him and his wife together. 8 Then the man and his wife become as one person. They are not separate; they are together as one person. 9 God has put them together to be husband and wife. So nobody should make them separate.'

10 When Jesus went into the house, the disciples* asked him about these things again. 11 So Jesus said to them, 'A man must not send his wife away and marry another woman. That is against God's rules. The man must not have sex with that other woman. 12 And a woman must not leave her husband and marry another man. That is also against God's rules. The woman must not have sex with the other man.'

Jesus prays for some children

13 People were bringing children to Jesus. They wanted him to put his hand on each child's head while he prayed for that child. The disciples* told the people that they should not bring their children. 14 But when Jesus saw this, he was angry. 'Do not stop the children', Jesus said to them. 'Let them come to me. People must be like these children so that God can rule their lives. 15 What I say is true. A person must be like a child when that person asks God to rule his life. If he does not become like a child, God will not rule his life.' 16 And Jesus hugged the children. Then he put his hands on each of them and he prayed for them.

Jesus meets a rich man

17 While Jesus went on his way, a man ran to meet him. He went down on his knees in front of Jesus. 'Good Teacher', he said to Jesus, 'what must I do so that I can live always?'

18 'I would like to know why you are calling me good', Jesus said to him. 'Only God is good. 19 And you know God's rules.

"Do not kill anyone.
Do not have sex with a woman who is not your wife.
Do not rob anyone.
Do not say things that are not true.
Do not take things that are not yours.
Love and obey your father and your mother." '

20 'Teacher', the man replied, 'I have done all these things since I was a young boy.'

21 Jesus looked at the man and Jesus loved him. 'There is still something else that you must do', Jesus said to him. 'Go. You must sell everything that you have. Give the money to poor people. Then you will have valuable things in God's home called heaven. And come to me. Be my disciple*.'

22 When the man heard that, he was sad. Because he was a very rich man, he went away sadly.

23 Jesus looked round and he said to his disciples*, 'It is very difficult for rich people to let God rule their lives.'

24 They were very surprised about Jesus' words. Then Jesus spoke again to them. 'Young people, it is very difficult for anyone to let God rule his life or her life. 25 The hole in a needle* is very small. The big animal called the camel cannot go through it. But it is even more difficult than that for a rich person to let God rule his life or her life.'

26 When his disciples* heard Jesus, they were even more surprised. And they said to each other, 'So perhaps God will not save anyone!'

27 Jesus looked at them and he replied, 'It is impossible for people to do this. But God can do it. God can do everything.'

28 'Look!' Peter said to Jesus. 'We left everything to become your disciples*.'

29 Jesus said, 'What I say is true. Some people have left their house. Or they have left their brothers or sisters. Or they have left their mother or their father. Or they have left their

children or their fields. They have done that because of me. And they have done it because of God's good news. ³⁰But God will give those people many things instead. He will give them 100 things now, in this world, for each thing that they have left. They will receive houses and brothers and sisters. They will receive mothers and children and fields. But in this world, people will be against them. In the future world, they will live always. ³¹But many people who are very important now will not be important then. And people who are not important now will be very important then.'

Jesus talks again about his death

³²Jesus and his disciples* were walking along the road towards Jerusalem. Jesus was walking in front of them all, and the disciples* were very surprised. The people who were following behind them were afraid. Jesus asked his 12 disciples* to come close to him again. And he began to tell them what would happen to him soon. ³³'Look!' he said to them. 'We are going to Jerusalem. There, someone will deliver the Son* of Man to the important priests* and to the teachers of God's rules. These men will decide that he must die. Then they will deliver him to people who are not Jews*. ³⁴They will laugh* at him. They will spit* on him. They will hit him with sticks. Then they will kill him. After three days, he will become alive again.'

James and John ask Jesus to do something for them

³⁵James and John, who were Zebedee's sons, came to Jesus. 'Teacher', they said, 'we want to ask for something. Please do it for us.'

³⁶'What do you want me to do?' Jesus asked them.

³⁷They said to him, 'When you are king, we want to sit on your right side and on your left side.'

³⁸'You do not understand what you are asking for', he said to them. 'People will cause troubles for me that are like a cup of very bad wine*. Can you drink it too? They will be as bad as

deep water that will cover me up to and over my head. Can you go to that place too?'

39 'Yes, we can do all that', said James and John. Jesus said to them, 'Your troubles will be like mine. They will be like a cup of bad wine* that you must drink. They will be as bad as water that will cover you up to and over your head. 40 But I cannot give you the seats on my right side or on my left side. God has chosen who will sit there. He has prepared those seats for them.'

41 When the other 10 disciples* knew about this, they were angry with James and John. 42 But Jesus asked the disciples* to come. Jesus said, 'You know the things that rulers do. They think that they rule over countries. So they do the things that masters do. And important people use their authority over people. 43 But you should not be like that. The person who wants to be great among you must be your servant. 44 Anyone who wants to be the most important person must work for you all. 45 Even the Son* of Man came to earth to be a servant. He did not come here to have servants who must work for him. He came to die so that many people can be free.'

Jesus causes a blind* man to see

46 Then Jesus and his disciples* arrived in Jericho. When they were leaving the city again, a large crowd followed them. A blind* man called Bartimaeus was sitting by the side of the road. He was asking people to give him money. He was the son of Timaeus.

47 Somebody told Bartimaeus that Jesus from Nazareth was walking past him. So he began to shout. He said, 'Jesus, you are the Son of David. Please be kind to me!'

48 Many people told Bartimaeus that he should be quiet. But he shouted even louder than before, 'Jesus, Son of David, please be kind to me!'

49 Jesus stopped walking and he said to the people, 'Ask the man to come here.' So the people said to the blind* man,

'Be brave. Stand up. Jesus is asking you to go to him.' ⁵⁰So
Bartimaeus threw away his coat. He jumped up and he came
to Jesus.

⁵¹Because of this, Jesus said to Bartimaeus, 'What do you
want me to do for you?'

The blind* man said to Jesus, 'Teacher, I want to see.'

⁵²'Go', Jesus said to him. 'You are well because you believed.'
Immediately, Bartimaeus could see and he followed Jesus
along the road.

11

Jesus rides into Jerusalem city

¹Jesus and his disciples* were coming near to Jerusalem. They
were almost at the villages called Bethphage and Bethany.
They were on the hill called the Mount* of Olives*. Then Jesus
sent two of his disciples*.

²'Go to the village that is in front of you', Jesus said to the two
disciples*. 'When you arrive at the village, you will immediately
find a young donkey*. Someone has tied it there. Nobody has
ever yet ridden on it. Undo the rope* and bring the donkey*
here. ³Someone may ask you, "Why are you doing this?" Say
to him, "The Master needs the donkey*. He will send it back
here soon."'

⁴So the two disciples* went. They found the young donkey*
in the street. Someone had tied it outside, by a door. So the
disciples* undid the rope*. ⁵Some people were standing there.
They said to the two disciples*, 'What are you doing? Why are
you undoing the donkey*'s rope*?' ⁶The disciples* answered
them. They repeated what Jesus had asked them to say.
The people then let them take the donkey* away. ⁷The two
disciples* brought the young donkey* to Jesus. They put their
coats on the back of the animal. Then Jesus sat on it. ⁸Many

people put their coats down on the road. Other people put down branches. They had cut those branches from the trees.

9 Many people went in front of Jesus, and other people followed him. All of them were shouting,
    'We ask you to save us!
    Great is the king who comes on behalf of the Lord*!
  10 Great will be the future government of our great
    King David!
    We ask you to save us powerfully!'

11 Jesus arrived in Jerusalem. He went to God*'s Great House and he looked at everything there. It was late in the day, so he went out of the city to Bethany. And the 12 disciples* went with him.

A tree without fruit

12 On the next day, they returned from Bethany. And Jesus was hungry. 13 He saw a fig* tree, which was a long way away. There were leaves on it. So he went to see if it had fruit on it. When he reached it, he found nothing except leaves. That was because it was not the right season for fruit. 14 So Jesus said to the tree, 'Nobody will ever eat fruit from you again.' And his disciples* heard this.

Jesus goes to God*'s Great House

15 When they arrived in Jerusalem, Jesus went to God*'s Great House. People were buying and selling things there. He caused them all to leave. Some people were supplying money there. He pushed over their tables. And he pushed over the seats of the men who sold birds.

16 Jesus would not let anyone carry things through there.
17 While he was teaching the people, Jesus said, 'The Bible says:
    "My house will be a place where people from all
        countries pray.
    But you have made it a place where robbers hide."'

18 The important priests* and the teachers of God's rules
heard this. And they thought about how they could kill him.
They were afraid of him. That was because all the crowd were
listening to him. And the things that he taught caused the
crowd to be very surprised.

19 When it was evening, Jesus and his disciples* went out of
the city.

The fig* tree is dead

20 The next morning, Jesus and his disciples* passed the
fig* tree. They saw that it was completely dead. 21 Peter
remembered what Jesus had said. So he said to Jesus,
'Teacher, look at that fig* tree. You said that it should die. And
it has died.'

22 So Jesus said to them, 'You must believe God. 23 What I say
is true. A person could say to this mountain, "Move and throw
yourself into the sea." He must not let other ideas come into
his mind. He must believe that those things will happen. If
he does believe it, those things will happen. 24 So I tell you
this. When you pray to ask God for anything, believe. Believe
that you have received that thing. If you do, you will have it.
25-26 When you stand to pray, forgive* other people. If you have
anything against anyone, forgive that person. If you do forgive
them, your Father God, in his home called heaven, will forgive
you. He will forgive you for the bad things that you have done.'

Jesus talks about his authority

27 Jesus and his disciples* arrived again in Jerusalem. Jesus was
walking about at God*'s Great House. The important priests*,
the teachers of God's rules and the important Jews* came to
Jesus. 28 'What authority do you have to do these things?' they
asked him. 'Who gave you the authority to do these things?'

29 'I will ask you one question', Jesus replied. 'You should
answer me. If you do that, I will answer you. And I will tell

you what authority I have to do these things. 30 John baptised*
people. Was his authority from God, or was it from men? Tell
me the answer.'

31 Then the Jewish* leaders talked with each other. They said,
'We could say that God gave John his authority. But, if we
say that, Jesus will say to us, "You should have believed him."
32 We do not want to say that men gave John his authority.'
They did not want to say it because they were afraid of the
crowd. All the people believed that John really was a special
servant of God.

33 So the Jewish* leaders answered Jesus and they said, 'We do
not know who gave John his authority.'

And Jesus said to them, 'You will not tell me. So I will not tell
you what authority I have to do these things.'

12

Jesus tells a story about a garden

1 Then Jesus began to speak to the important Jews* again.
He told them stories. He said, 'There was a man who made a
garden. He planted vines* there and he planted strong bushes
round them. He prepared a place where he could make the
grapes* into wine*. He also made a tall building. Then the man
found some men who would work for him. And he went away
to another country.

2 When it was time to cut the grapes*, the man sent a servant
to the workers. The man wanted the workers to give him some
fruit from the garden. 3 But the workers took the servant and
they hit him with sticks. They sent him away with nothing. 4 So
the man sent another servant to the workers. They hit this
servant on the head. And they did other bad things to him. 5 The
man then sent another servant, but the farmers killed this
servant. He sent many other servants. The workers hit some
servants with sticks. And the workers killed some servants.

⁶The man had only one person that he could still send. This was his own son, and the man loved him very much. So, last of all, he sent his son to the workers. That was because he said, "The workers know that my son is important."

⁷But those workers said to each other, "This son will receive the garden from his father. We should kill the son and then the garden will be ours." ⁸The workers took the son and they killed him. Then they threw his dead body out of the garden.'

⁹'I will tell you what the master of the garden will do', said Jesus. 'He will come and he will kill the workers. He will give the garden to other people.'

¹⁰'I am sure that you have read these words in the Bible:
    "The builders did not want to use a certain stone.
      But that stone became the most important stone at
        the corner.
  ¹¹ The Lord* God did this.
      And we can see that he did something great."'

¹²The leaders wanted to put Jesus in a prison. They knew that he had told this story about them. But they were afraid of the crowd. So, they left him and they went away.

The Pharisees* ask about the money that Caesar* demanded

¹³Then the leaders sent some Pharisees* to Jesus. They also sent some men who wanted to obey King Herod. They tried to use Jesus' words to cause trouble for him. ¹⁴These men came to Jesus. 'Teacher', they said, 'we know that you only say true things. It does not matter to you what other people think. You do not change your answers if someone is important. You really do teach us what God wants us to do. So should we pay money to Caesar* (the Roman* ruler), or should we not? ¹⁵Should we give that money, or not?'

Jesus knew that those men were not honest. So he said, 'You should not ask that question to cause trouble for me. Bring me a coin. I want to see it.' 16 So they brought it. And Jesus said to them, 'Whose picture is on this coin? Whose name is on it?'

They replied, 'It is Caesar*'s picture, and Caesar*'s name.'

17 So Jesus said to them, 'So give to Caesar* the things that are his. And give to God the things that are God's.'

They were very surprised.

The Sadducees* ask Jesus a question

18 Also, some Sadducees* came to Jesus. Sadducees do not believe that anyone can become alive again after death. They asked Jesus about this.

19 'Teacher', they said to Jesus, 'Moses wrote these things for us in our rules. If a man dies without children, his brother must marry the man's wife. And then their children will be called the children of the brother who died. 20 At one time, there were 7 brothers. The oldest brother married a woman. But he died without children. 21 So the second brother married her. He also died without children. Then the third brother married this woman. 22 And the same thing happened to all 7 brothers. They had no children. After this, the woman also died. 23 You teach that at some time dead people will live again. On that day, whose wife will that woman be? She married all 7 brothers.'

24 'You are very wrong', Jesus said to the Sadducees*. 'This is because you do not know the Bible. And you do not know how powerful God is. 25 At some time, people who have died will become alive again. But then men and women will not marry. They will not have husbands or wives. Instead, they will be like the angels* in God's home. 26 But God does make dead people alive again. You should have read what Moses wrote. See the chapter about the bush. There, God spoke to Moses and God said, "I am the God of Abraham. I am the God of Isaac. And I am the God of Jacob." 27 God is not the God of people who

are dead. He is the God of people who are alive. So you are
very wrong.'

Jesus teaches people about the most important rule

28 One of the teachers of God's rules came near. He heard
Jesus' conversations with the leaders. The teacher knew that
Jesus had answered them well. So the teacher asked Jesus,
'Which rule is the most important among God's rules?'

29 'This rule is the most important rule', replied Jesus. 'Listen,
everyone from Israel*'s families*. The Lord*, our God, is the
only Lord*. 30 And you must love the Lord*, your God. Love him
with all your mind. Love him with all your life. Love him with
all your thoughts. Love him with all that you do. 31 The second
most important rule is this: You must love other people as
much as you love yourself. No other rules are as important as
these two.'

32 The teacher of God's rules said to Jesus, 'Teacher, you
answered well. You are right to say that the Lord* is the only
God. And there is no other God except him. 33 We must love
him with all our mind. We must love him with all that we learn.
We must love him with all that we do. We must also love other
people as much as we love ourselves. This is more important
than all the gifts or animals that we offer to God.'

34 Jesus heard that the man had answered well. So Jesus said
to him, 'You are almost ready for God to rule your life.' After
that, everybody was afraid to ask Jesus any more questions.

Jesus teaches the people about the Messiah*

35 Jesus was teaching the people at God*'s Great House. He
said, 'The teachers of God's rules talk about the Messiah*. And
they say that he is King David's son. Think about this. 36 The
Holy* Spirit helped David himself to write:
      "The Lord* said to my Lord*:
      Sit at my right side until I win completely against
         your enemies.

You will even be able to put your feet on them."

37 David himself calls the Messiah*" Lord*". So we should not say that the Messiah* is only David's son.'

The large crowd liked to listen to the things that Jesus was saying.

38 While Jesus was teaching the people, he said, 'Be careful about the teachers of God's rules. They want people to think that they are important. So they walk about in long clothes. They like it if people recognise them in the market place. 39 They want the best seats in the meeting places. They choose the most important places at special meals. 40 These men take everything away from women after their husbands have died, even their houses. Then they pray for a long time so that other people will hear them. God will punish* those men very much because of these things.'

Jesus talks about people who give to God

41 The crowd were giving their gifts for God*'s Great House. They threw their coins into a box. Jesus sat near the box and he watched them. Many rich people put a lot of money into the box. 42 But then a woman came. Her husband had died and she was poor. She put in two coins that had very small value.

43 Jesus asked his disciples* to come to him. 'What I say is true', he said to them. 'This poor woman has put a better gift into the box than all the other people have put in. 44 All those rich people only put a part of their money into the box. And they have plenty of money. This woman has nothing. But she put in all the money that she had. She has put in all the money that she needs to live.'

13

Jesus talks about future events

¹Then Jesus left God*'s Great House. While he was leaving, one of his disciples* said to him, 'Teacher, look at the large stones that are in the walls of God's House. The buildings are very strong!'

²Jesus said to him, 'Look at all these large buildings! Enemies will completely destroy them. They will throw down every stone that is on top of another stone.'

³After that, Jesus was sitting on the hill called the Mount* of Olives*. He could look across at God*'s Great House. Peter, James, John and Andrew went together to talk with him. The crowd was not there. ⁴'Please tell us when these things will happen', they said. 'What will we see just before all these things happen?'

⁵Jesus began to say to them, 'Be careful! Some people will tell you things that are not true. Do not believe those people. ⁶Many people will say that they have come on my behalf. They will say, "I am here!" Many people will believe their false words. ⁷People will tell you about wars. And there will be reports about wars. Do not be afraid. Those things must happen, but that is not yet the end. ⁸People in one country will attack the people in another country. Kings and their armies will fight against other kings and their armies. The ground will move in many different places. Some people will be without food. These things are like the first pains before a baby is born.

⁹So, be careful! People will take you to their rulers. People will hit you in the meeting places. People will bring you to stand in front of kings and in front of rulers. You will be there on my behalf. And you will tell them about me. ¹⁰And you must first tell the good news to people in every country. ¹¹People will take you away and they will bring you to their leaders. But do not be afraid about the words that you should say. You should

say the words that God puts into your mind at that time. You will not be speaking your own words. Those words will come into your mind from the Holy* Spirit.

¹²A man will send his own brother to die. A father will send his own child to die. Children will be against their parents and they will ask rulers to kill their parents. ¹³All people will be cruel to you because you are mine. But God will save the person who waits patiently until the end.

¹⁴There will be a time when you will see a very bad thing. It is the very bad thing that destroys. It will stand where it should not be. (When you read this, you must understand it.) When you see this thing, people in Judea must run to the hills to hide. ¹⁵A person who is on his roof must not go down into his house. He must not stop to get anything from his home. ¹⁶A person who is in a field must not go back to his home. He must not return to pick up his coat.

¹⁷That time will be bad for women who are hoping to have a baby soon. And that time will be bad for those women who are trying to give milk to their babies. ¹⁸You must pray to God that these troubles will not happen in winter. ¹⁹Very bad troubles will happen to people. Nothing as bad as those troubles has ever happened since God made the world. Nothing as bad as those troubles will ever happen again after that time. ²⁰The Lord* God will cause those days of very bad trouble to be less. If he did not do that, there would be nobody still alive. But God will cause those days to be less. He will do that to help the people that he has chosen. ²¹Someone may say to you then, "Look, here is the Messiah*!" Or they may say, "Look, he is there!" Do not believe them. ²²Some people will say to you, "I am the Messiah*." Other people will say, "I am a special messenger* from God." But their words are false. They will do powerful things. Those things will surprise everyone very much. If possible, they would even cause the people that God has chosen to believe them. ²³So be careful! I have told you about all these things before they happen.

The time when the Son* of Man returns

24 Then, after all these bad things have happened, the sun will become dark. And the moon will not shine. 25 Stars will fall out of the sky. And the powerful things in the sky will leave their usual places.

26 Then people will see the Son* of Man. He will come in the clouds. He will be very powerful and very beautiful. 27 Then he will send the angels*. And they will bring together all the people that God has chosen. The angels* will bring them from every direction. And God's people will come from every part of God's home and from every part of earth.

A lesson about the fig* tree

28 Here is a lesson about the fig* tree. When the new branches on the tree start to grow, the leaves appear. Then you know that the summer will begin soon. 29 So you will see that these things are happening. And then you will know that the Son* of Man will come soon. He will be like someone at the door who is ready to come in. 30 What I say to you is true. The people who are alive will not all die first. Some of them will not die until all these things have happened. 31 The earth and the sky will have an end. But my words will never have an end.

Nobody knows when the Son* of Man will return to the world

32 Nobody knows the day or the hour when all these things will happen. Even the angels* who are in God's home do not know. Even the Son does not know. Only God the Father knows when they will happen. 33 Watch carefully! You do not know when all these things will happen. So keep yourselves ready. 34 It is like when a master begins a journey. Before he leaves his house, he gives authority to his servants. He tells each servant about the work that he should do. Then he tells the servant at the door to be ready for his master's return.

35 And you do not know when the master of the house will return. So keep yourselves ready and watch carefully. He might arrive in the evening, or in the middle of the night. Or he might arrive early in the morning, or just before the sun rises. 36 He may surprise you and he may find you asleep. 37 I am saying this to you. And I am also saying this to everyone else. Keep yourselves ready!'

14

The important priests* and the teachers of God's rules want to kill Jesus

1 It was now two days before the Passover* and the days when the Jews* eat flat bread. The important priests* and the teachers of God's rules wanted to kill Jesus. But they wanted to take him away secretly. So they tried to decide how they could do that. 2 'We do not want to do it during the Passover*', they said to each other. 'The people will be angry. And they may fight against us if we do that.'

A woman pours expensive oil on Jesus' head

3 While Jesus was in Bethany, he went to Simon's house. People called that man, 'Simon with the illness in his skin'. While Jesus was eating a meal, a woman came into the house. She brought a small stone jar that contained expensive oil with a lovely smell. The person who made that oil had used only one plant. It was the plant called nard. The woman broke the jar to open it. And then she poured the oil over Jesus' head.

4 But some people became angry. 'This woman should not have wasted the oil', they said to each other. 5 'She should have sold it and she should have given the money to poor people. She could have sold it for more than 300 coins. A man would have to work for a year to get that much money.' So, they spoke angrily to the woman.

⁶But Jesus said, 'Do not speak to her like that! Do not cause trouble for her. She has done a good thing to me. ⁷You will always have poor people with you. You can help them at any time that you want. But you will not always have me with you. ⁸She did what she was able to do. She poured oil over my body to prepare it. So now, my body is ready for people to bury me. ⁹What I say to you is true. Everywhere, people will tell other people about God's good news. At the same time, they will also tell those people about the thing that this woman did. And so they will remember her.'

Judas agrees to help the important priests*

¹⁰Then Judas Iscariot went to the important priests*. He said that he would help them to catch Jesus. (Judas was one of the 12 disciples*.) ¹¹The important priests* were very happy about this. And they promised to give him money. Then Judas watched for the right moment for him to give Jesus to them.

Jesus eats his last meal with his 12 disciples*

¹²It was now the first day of the whole week when the Jews* eat flat bread. On this day, each family would kill a young sheep for the Passover* meal. Jesus' disciples* said to him, 'We will go to prepare the Passover* meal for you. Where do you want us to do that?'

¹³So Jesus sent two disciples*. 'Go into the city', he said to them. 'A man, who is carrying a jar of water, will meet you. Follow him. ¹⁴He will go to a house. And you must say to the master of that house, "The Teacher sends this message to you: 'Where is the room for visitors where I can eat the Passover* meal with my disciples*?' " ¹⁵Then the man will show you a large room upstairs. The room will have in it all the things that you will need. You should prepare the Passover* meal for us there.'

¹⁶ Then the two disciples* left and they went into the city. They found everything as Jesus had told them. So, they prepared the Passover* meal there.

¹⁷ When it was evening, Jesus arrived with the 12 disciples*. ¹⁸ While they were eating the meal, Jesus said, 'What I say to you is true. One of you will help the Jewish* rulers to take me away. It is someone who is eating this meal with me.'

¹⁹ The disciples* became very sad. Each one of them said to Jesus, 'I hope that you do not mean me!'

²⁰ 'It is one of the 12 disciples*. That man is putting his bread into the same dish as I am', Jesus said to them.

²¹ 'The Son* of Man must go, as the Bible says', Jesus said. 'But it will be very bad for that man who helps to lead the Son* of Man away. It would have been a better thing for that man if he had never been born.'

The Passover* meal

²² While Jesus and his disciples* were eating, he took a loaf. He thanked God for it. Then he broke the bread and he gave the pieces to them. 'Take this bread and eat it', he said to them. 'This is my body.'

²³ Then Jesus took a cup. He thanked God. Then he gave the cup to them and they all drank from it.

²⁴ 'This is my blood', he said to them. 'It shows that there is a promise from God. When I die, my blood will leave my body. And so God will save many people. ²⁵ What I say is true. I will not drink wine* again until God begins to rule his people. And then I will drink the new wine*.'

²⁶ Then Jesus and his disciples* sang a song to God. Then they went out. They went to the hill that people call the Mount* of Olives*.

Jesus tells the disciples* what will happen

27Then Jesus said to them, 'Tonight's events will cause you all
to do wrong things. The Bible says:
    "I will kill the man who leads the sheep.
    And the sheep will run away in different directions."

28But I will become alive again. Then I will go before you
to Galilee.'

29Peter said to Jesus, 'Even if everyone else does wrong things,
I will not leave you.'

30'What I say to you is true', Jesus replied to Peter. 'Tonight,
you will say three times that you do not know me. You will do it
before the cockerel* makes its noise for the second time.'

31But Peter answered Jesus strongly, 'If necessary, I will die
with you. But I will never tell anyone that I do not know you.'
All the other disciples* said the same thing.

Jesus prays in the garden called Gethsemane

32Then they arrived at a garden called Gethsemane. Jesus said
to his disciples*, 'Sit here while I pray.' 33Then Jesus took Peter,
James and John with him. He started to feel that troubles
were filling his mind. 34'I am very sad. I could die because I
feel so sad. Wait here and keep awake', Jesus said to them.

35Jesus went a short way in front of them. He went down on
the ground. He prayed that, if possible, God would save him
from the events of that time. 36He said, 'Abba, (my Father),
you can do anything. Please take this pain away from me. But I
do not ask you to do what I want. I choose what you want.'

37Jesus returned and he found Peter, James and John. They
were sleeping. He said to Peter, 'Simon, you are asleep! You
could not keep awake for even one hour! 38You must keep
awake and you must pray. If you do not do that, you might do

the wrong thing. You really want to do the right thing, but it is too difficult for you.'

³⁹Jesus went away again and he prayed again. He said the same words to God. ⁴⁰Jesus returned again to Peter, James and John. He saw that they were sleeping. They could not keep their eyes open. They did not know what to say to him.

⁴¹When Jesus returned the third time, he said to them, 'You should not be sleeping and resting. You have slept enough. This is the hour. Look! See the man who is helping bad men to take the Son* of Man away. ⁴²Stand up; we are going. Look! Here is the man who will help them to take me away.'

Judas leads the men who will take Jesus away

⁴³Jesus was still speaking when, immediately, Judas arrived. He was one of Jesus' 12 disciples*. A crowd came with him. They were carrying long sharp knives and heavy sticks. The important priests*, the teachers of God's rules and the leaders had sent these men.

⁴⁴Before this, Judas had said to these men, 'I will kiss one of the men. That is the man that you must take away. Lead him away and do not let him go.' ⁴⁵When they arrived, Judas went immediately to Jesus. 'Teacher', he said to Jesus. Then he kissed Jesus in a friendly way. ⁴⁶So the men took hold of Jesus. ⁴⁷But a certain man who was standing there took his long sharp knife. And he used it against the servant of the most important priest*. He cut off the servant's ear.

⁴⁸Then Jesus spoke to the crowd. 'You have come with long sharp knives and with heavy sticks to take me away', he said. 'That is how you would take a robber away. But you know that I am not a robber. ⁴⁹I was with you every day at God*'s Great House when I was teaching the people. You did not take me away then. But the things that are in the Bible must happen.' ⁵⁰Then all Jesus' disciples* left him and they ran away.

⁵¹A certain young man was following Jesus. He was only wearing one piece of cloth over his whole body. The men tried to take hold of this young man. ⁵²But the young man left the piece of cloth behind, and he ran away. When he ran away, he was not wearing anything.

The most important priest* asks Jesus questions

⁵³The men took Jesus to the most important priest*. All the important priests* met, with the leaders and with the teachers of God's rules.

⁵⁴Peter followed Jesus. But he did not go near Jesus. So Peter went into the yard outside the house of the most important priest*. He sat down with the guards*. Peter kept himself warm by the fire.

⁵⁵The important priests* and everyone at the meeting wanted Jesus to die. So they tried to find some men who could say things against Jesus. But they did not find anyone who could help them. ⁵⁶Many people said things about Jesus. But they were saying things that were not true. And they did not agree with each other.

⁵⁷Then some men stood up and they said something else about Jesus. But their words were also not true. ⁵⁸They said, 'We heard Jesus say, "I will destroy God*'s Great House, which men have built. In three days, I will build another House for God. It will not be men who build this new house." ' ⁵⁹Even then, these people who were speaking against Jesus did not say the same thing.

⁶⁰Then the most important priest* stood up in the middle and he spoke to Jesus. 'You should reply now. These people have said that you have done many bad things. What do you say about this?' ⁶¹But Jesus did not reply. He did not say anything.

So again, the most important priest* asked Jesus, 'Are you the Messiah*? Are you the Son of God?'

62 'I am', Jesus replied. 'And you will all see the Son* of Man. He will be sitting at the right side of God, who is most powerful. And he will come with the clouds of God's home, which is called heaven.'

63 The most important priest* tore his own clothes. 'We do not need anyone else to tell us about Jesus', he said. 64 'You have heard the bad words that he has spoken against God. What do you decide?'

Everyone agreed that Jesus should die.

65 Then some of the men began to spit* on Jesus. They covered his eyes and they hit him. They said, 'Speak God's words, if you can!' Then the guards* slapped Jesus while they were taking him away.

Peter says three times that he does not know Jesus

66 Peter was still outside in the yard. One of the young women who worked for the most important priest* came. 67 She saw Peter, who was making himself warm by the fire.

She looked at him and she said, 'You also were with Jesus, the man from Nazareth.'

68 'That is not true!' he replied. 'I do not know what you are talking about! I do not understand what you mean!' Then Peter walked to the gate of the house.

69 The young woman saw him, and again she began to say to the other people there, 'This man is one of the men who were with Jesus.' 70 But Peter again said that it was not true.

After some time, the other people who were standing there said to Peter, 'You are from Galilee. So we are sure that you were with Jesus.'

71 Peter began to speak strongly to them. 'I do not know this man that you are talking about', he said. And Peter asked God to punish* him if his words were not true. 72 Immediately,

the cockerel* made its noise for a second time. Then Peter remembered what Jesus had said to him: 'You will say three times that you do not know me. You will do it before the cockerel* makes its noise for the second time.'

When Peter thought about this, he wept.

15

Pilate asks Jesus questions

¹Immediately in the morning, all the important people had a meeting. The important priests* met with the leaders, the teachers of God's rules, and the other important people. They tied Jesus and they led him away. They brought him to Pilate.

²Pilate asked Jesus, 'Are you the king of the Jews*?'

Jesus replied, 'Yes, it is as you say.'

³Then the important priests* said to Pilate that Jesus had done many bad things. ⁴So Pilate asked him again, 'What is your answer? You should say something! Listen! They are saying that you have done many bad things.'

⁵Jesus still did not answer him. And Pilate was very surprised about that.

⁶Each year during the Passover*, Pilate let one person go out of the prison. The people had to ask him for the person that they wanted. ⁷A man called Barabbas was in the prison at that time. He and some other men had fought against the government. And they had killed someone when they were fighting. ⁸The crowd came to Pilate. And they asked Pilate to do what he usually did.

⁹Pilate answered the people, 'Do you want me to make the king of the Jews* free for you?' ¹⁰Pilate knew why the important priests* had brought Jesus to him. The people seemed to like Jesus more than they liked the priests*. And that had made the priests angry. ¹¹But the important priests* talked strongly to

the people. They told the people that they should ask Pilate to make Barabbas free instead.

12 So Pilate again asked the crowd, 'So what should I do to Jesus? He is the man that you call "the king of the Jews*". '

13 The people shouted again. They shouted, 'Kill him on a cross*!'

14 'Why should I kill him on a cross*?' Pilate asked. 'What bad things has he done?'

But the people shouted even louder, 'Kill him on a cross*!'

15 Pilate decided to do what the crowd wanted. So he made Barabbas free for them. He told his soldiers that they should take Jesus away. They should hit him many times with a whip*. Then they should put him on a cross* to die.

16 Then the soldiers took Jesus to the yard at the ruler's house. And they told all the soldiers in their group that they must come. 17 Then they put a dark red coat on Jesus. They made a crown* out of sharp branches, and they put it on his head.

18 Then the soldiers began to shout to Jesus, 'Oh yes, King of the Jews*!' 19 The soldiers took a stick and they hit Jesus on the head with it. They spat* on him. Then they went down on their knees in front of him. They told him how great he was. 20 But they were laughing* at him. Then they took off the dark red coat. They put Jesus' own clothes back on him. Then they led him towards the place where they would put him on the cross*.

The soldiers put Jesus on a cross*

21 A man called Simon was walking past Jesus and the soldiers. He was coming in from outside the city. The soldiers told Simon that he must carry Jesus' cross*. Simon was from the city called Cyrene. He was the father of Alexander and Rufus. 22 The soldiers brought Jesus to the place that was called Golgotha. (Golgotha means 'the place of a skull*'.)

23 They gave Jesus some wine* to drink. They had put some medicine called myrrh into the wine*. But Jesus would not drink the wine*. 24 Then the soldiers put Jesus on the cross*. They took his clothes for themselves. They played a game to decide which soldier would get each of his clothes.

25 It was 9 o'clock when the soldiers fixed Jesus to the cross*. 26 Above his head, they put a notice to say why they were punishing* him. The notice said, 'The King of the Jews*'. 27 They also put two robbers on crosses* with Jesus. One robber was on the right side of Jesus. And the other robber was on his left side. 28 [The Bible says that this would happen. And it did happen. The Bible says, 'People included him with people who did not obey God's rules.']

29 The people who walked by moved their heads from one side to the other side. And they said bad things to Jesus. They said to him, 'Oh! You said that you would destroy God*'s Great House. And you said that in three days you would build it again. 30 If you can really do that, save yourself. Come down from the cross*!'

31 The important priests* and the teachers of God's rules laughed* about him to each other. 'This man saved other people. But he cannot save himself. 32 If he is the Messiah*, the king of Israel, he should come down from the cross* now. We would see it and then we would believe.' The two men who were on the crosses* next to Jesus also said bad things to him.

Jesus dies

33 At midday, the whole country became dark. It continued to be dark until 3 o'clock. 34 At 3 o'clock, Jesus shouted loudly, 'Eloi, Eloi, lama sabachthani.' That means, 'My God, my God, I want to know why you have left me alone!'

35 Some people were standing near his cross* and they heard him. They said, 'Look! He is asking Elijah to come.'

36 One man ran to get a soft cloth. He poured bad wine* on it.
And he put it on the end of a stick. Then he lifted it up to Jesus
so that he could drink the wine* from it. 'Wait!' he said. 'We
will see if Elijah comes to take Jesus down from the cross*.'

37 Then Jesus shouted loudly again and after that, he died.

38 And someone or something tore the curtain inside God*'s
Great House completely into two parts from the top down.

39 The captain of the soldiers was standing in front of Jesus.
He saw how Jesus died. 'It is true', he said. 'This man was the
Son of God.'

40 Some women were also there. They were not very near the
cross*. But they were watching all these events. Mary, from
the town called Magdala, was among the women. Another
woman called Mary was also there. She was the mother of
the younger James and Joses. Salome was also there. 41 These
women had been Jesus' disciples* when he was in Galilee.
There, they had helped him. And many other women were
there who had come to Jerusalem with him.

Joseph buries Jesus' dead body

42 It would soon be Friday evening. The Jews* were preparing
for Saturday, when they rested. 43 A man called Joseph went
to see Pilate. Joseph was from a town called Arimathea. He
was a good man and he was an important leader of the Jews*.
He was waiting for the time when God would start to rule
his people. Joseph bravely asked Pilate for the dead body of
Jesus. 44 Pilate was surprised that Jesus had already died. He
asked the captain of the soldiers to come to him. Then he
asked him when Jesus had died. 45 The captain told Pilate that
Jesus was dead. So then Pilate let Joseph have Jesus' dead
body. 46 Joseph bought a new piece of soft white cloth. He took
Jesus down from the cross*. He put the cloth round him. And
he buried him in a large hole that Joseph's workers had cut

into the rock. After this, he rolled a very big stone in front of the hole.

⁴⁷Mary from the town called Magdala, and Mary, the mother of Joses, were watching. They saw where Joseph had put Jesus' dead body.

16

Jesus becomes alive again

¹After the day for rest had finished, the women bought some seeds with a beautiful smell. They wanted to put those seeds and some oil on Jesus' body. These women were Mary from Magdala, Salome, and Mary the mother of James. ²They went out very early in the morning on the first day of the week (Sunday). The sun was just rising. They went to the hole in the rock where Joseph had buried Jesus' dead body.

³The women asked each other, 'Who will roll the big stone away for us? It is in front of the hole in the rock where they buried Jesus.'

⁴They looked and they saw the stone. It was a very big stone. But someone had already rolled it away from the hole. ⁵When the women went into the hole in the rock, they saw a young man. He was sitting on the right side of the place. He wore long white clothes. They were very afraid.

⁶The young man said to them, 'Do not be afraid. You are looking for Jesus from Nazareth. The soldiers killed him on a cross*, but he has become alive again. He is not here. Look! You can see the place where the men put him. ⁷But you must go to tell his disciples* and Peter about this. Tell them that Jesus is going before you to Galilee. There you will see him, as he told you.'

⁸The women went out of the hole in the rock. They ran away from there. They felt afraid and confused. They did not say anything to anyone, because they were afraid.

9 Jesus became alive again early on the first day of the week, Sunday. He appeared first to Mary from Magdala. Jesus had caused 7 bad spirits* to leave her. 10 She went to the people who had been with Jesus. They were all very sad and they were crying. Mary spoke to them. 11 She told them that Jesus was alive. And she told them that she had seen him. But they did not believe it.

12 After these things had happened, Jesus appeared to two other disciples*. They were walking away from the town. He seemed to be different to them. 13 Those two disciples* went and they told all the other disciples*. But the other disciples* also did not believe them.

14 After that, Jesus appeared to the 11 disciples* while they were eating. He told them that they were wrong not to believe. They should have changed their minds. People had seen that he was alive. But the disciples* did not believe them.

15 And Jesus said to them, 'Go to all people everywhere in the world. Tell God's good news to everyone. 16 If a person believes, then you should baptise* that person. And God will save that person. But if a person does not believe, God will be that person's judge*. And he will punish* that person. 17 These powerful things will happen after people believe. On my behalf, they will send bad spirits* out of people. They will speak new languages. 18 If they pick up a snake, it will not hurt them. If they drink poison, it will not hurt them. They will put their hands on ill people, and God will make those people well.'

Jesus goes up to God's home called heaven

19 So, after the Lord* Jesus had spoken to them, God took him up into God's home. And Jesus sat down at the right side of God.

20 But the disciples* went out everywhere. They told people God's good news. The Lord* worked with them. And the Lord* did powerful things to show that their message was true.

WORD LIST

AD years after Jesus was born.

angel one of God's special servants in God's home. Angels
   bring messages from God.

apostle a special disciple* of Jesus. These men had a special
   job to do for him. God sent them to teach other people
   about Jesus.

baptise John baptised the people who came to him. The people
   were sorry for all the wrong things that they had done. And
   they wanted to obey God. So they asked John to baptise
   them. John used water from the river Jordan to do this.
   Today, we baptise people who become Christians. In some
   churches, the person must bathe his whole body. In other
   churches, the water goes only on the person's head. And
   in some churches, Christians also baptise children who are
   born into Christian families.

baptism the event when someone baptises* a person.

Baptist John was called John the Baptist because he
   baptised* people.

BC years before Jesus was born.

blind a blind person cannot see.

Caesar the most important Roman* ruler. He lived in the city
   called Rome.

camel a large animal like a horse that can live in dry places. It
   can carry heavy things on its back.

carpenter a carpenter is a man who works with wood.

cockerel male of a bird called a hen.

cross someone fastened one piece of wood across another
   piece of wood. This made a cross. The Roman* soldiers fixed
   people to crosses to kill them.

crown a special hat that a king wears on his head; or, a hat
   that is like a king's crown.

disciple someone who wants to do the same things as another
    person and who wants to learn from him. At that time, the
    disciple usually travelled with his teacher and he worked for
    his teacher.

donkey an animal like a small horse.

enemy a person who wants to hurt or to attack.

family family included father, mother and children; sometimes
    it means father, grandfathers and those who had been born
    before them.

fast when you decide not to eat any food for a certain time.

fig a fruit that is good to eat.

forgive, forgiven not to remember wrong things that a person
    has done; to choose not to punish* someone for wrong
    things that the person has done. God forgives us for the
    wrong things that we have done. He chooses to do this, but
    we must change our minds. We must ask him to come into
    our lives.

God's Great House the special big building in Jerusalem usually
    called the temple. There people prayed and they gave gifts
    to God. Only priests* went into the building. Other people
    went into the yards that were there.

grape a fruit that people eat or they make it into wine*.

guard a guard keeps things or places or people safe; or he is
    like a policeman who takes people away.

guilty when we have done wrong things, we are guilty.

hell the place where God sends some people after they die.
    People are very sad there because of their pains and
    troubles. It is a place for people who did not want to believe
    in Jesus during their lives.

holy special for God.

Holy Spirit The Holy Spirit is God, even as the Father and the
    Son are God. But there is only one God. The Holy Spirit is
    always working in this world. He helps people to believe.
    He teaches them. And he is present in the lives of people
    who believe.

honey honey is very sweet. An insect called a bee makes honey.

hypocrites hypocrites say that they do one thing. But really,
   they do something different. They want people to think that
   they are good. But, really, they are bad people.
Israel all the people in the families* of Abraham, Isaac and
   Jacob. God chose Israel to be his special people. The word
   can also mean the country that God gave to these people.
Jew a person who is born from the families* of Abraham, Isaac
   and Jacob.
Jewish a word that describes a Jew* or anything that is for
   the Jews*.
judge to say what is right or wrong, good or bad. A judge is
   a person with authority to say if another person is right
   or wrong.
lamp a light to use in a house.
laugh at, laugh about to laugh against someone to cause
   him to feel bad; to laugh when a person says cruel things
   about someone.
life perhaps ' soul*'. The same word in the Greek language
   can mean 'life' or ' soul*'. We are not sure which is the right
   English word in Mark 8:35-37.
Lord a name for God and for Jesus. The word means 'master'.
   But it also translates God's name from the language called
   Hebrew. And in that language, God's name may mean 'He is
   always God.'
messenger a person who brings a message to other people.
Messiah God said that he would send a special person to save
   his people. That person was called the Messiah. Jesus is this
   person. The word 'Christ' is a translation of 'Messiah'.
Mount of Olives a hill near Jerusalem city where many olive*
   trees grow.
needle a thin sharp piece of bone or metal. It has a small hole
   at one end. People use it when they make clothes.
net people use many thin ropes* to make something like a very
   big bag with small holes in it. People use a net to catch fish
   or birds.
olive a tree with small fruits; or the fruits themselves.

Passover an important holiday for the Jews*. Each family eats a special meal on this day every year. They remember that God helped the Jews* to leave Egypt. They were slaves in Egypt and Moses led them away.

Pharisees a group of Jews*. Pharisees went to a special school to learn God's rules. They tried to obey all God's rules. But many Pharisees did not like the things that Jesus taught.

power a person who has power can do powerful things.

priest a man who offered gifts to God on behalf of other people. The Jews* had priests who worked in God*'s Great House.

prophet a person who tells people messages from God. He is a special servant of God.

punish to cause someone pain. Usually, it is because that person has done wrong things.

Roman a person or a thing from the city called Rome.

rope a long thin piece of strong material. People use ropes to tie things together.

Sabbath the day when the Jews* rested. It started on Friday at sunset. They did no work until Saturday at sunset.

Sadducees a group of Jews* who did not believe that dead people could become alive again.

Satan the bad spirit* that God sent away from God's home a long time ago; he is the leader of all the bad spirits*.

skull the largest bone inside the head.

soil the top part of the ground. Plants grow in it.

Son of Man the name that Jesus used when he talked about himself. This name appears in the books of Daniel and Ezekiel.

soul a part of a person that we cannot see. Our soul is in us while we are alive. It continues to live after we die.

spirit another part of a person that is alive, but which we cannot see. There are also good spirits. They are like angels*. The Holy* Spirit is God's Spirit. There are also bad spirits.

spit, spat to send water out of the mouth.

tongue the large red part of the body in the mouth; it helps us
to speak.

vine a plant that has fruit called grapes*.

wheat a plant that has many seeds. It grows on farms. People
make flour with the seeds. And they bake it to make bread.

whip soldiers used a whip to hit people. It had long narrow
pieces of leather. There were pieces of metal on the ends.
The whip caused a lot of pain.

wilderness a wilderness is a place where there are not many
plants. Not many people live there.

wine a drink that people make from grapes*. It has alcohol
in it.

wineskin a kind of bag. People did not then have bottles for
wine*. So they kept the wine* in wineskins. People made
them from the skin of animals.

worm a small, thin animal that lives under the ground. Some
worms eat dead things.

yeast people put yeast into flour and water when they want
to make bread. The yeast grows and it causes the flour to
become bigger. Then it is more like a loaf of bread. Then you
can bake the bread and you can eat it.

zealot an enemy of the Roman* government. The zealots were
a group of people who fought against the Romans* in Israel*.